Original title:
The Ocean's Silent Song

Copyright © 2025 Creative Arts Management OÜ
All rights reserved.

Author: Evelyn Hartman
ISBN HARDBACK: 978-1-80587-332-7
ISBN PAPERBACK: 978-1-80587-802-5

Gentle Ripples of Remembrance

In a sea of socks lost at play,
Waves tickle toes that have gone astray.
Seagulls gossip, plotting the lunch,
While crabs do a curious, sideways crunch.

Flip-flops parade with a clumsy flair,
As salty breezes toss up your hair.
Mollusks chuckle in their shells so snug,
While fish throw a party—give them a hug!

Melodies of the Maritime

A fish in a tux, it winks with glee,
Swaying to rhythms, under a sea spree.
The octopus jams on its glittery drum,
While jellyfish dance, looking quite numb.

A crab on the sax, playing groovy tunes,
With seahorses swinging beneath the blue moons.
The shrimp hold a chorus, all shouting hooray,
As dolphins join in, with flips and ballet!

Underwater Serenade

Coral reefs hum, a tickle and tease,
With clownfish laughing, doing the sneeze.
A turtle in shades, so cool and so wise,
Claims he can outswim the fastest of guys.

Starfish applaud with their five little arms,
While mermaids brag of their many charms.
The sea cucumbers join in the fun,
With jokes about crabs, one after one!

The Tranquil Blue

A whale with a hat sings a song so clear,
While shrimp in a line say, "What's in the beer?"
Seashells chime in, creating a ring,
As clams hold a feast, and the seaweed swings.

The starfish run polls on who swims the best,
While otters float by, just taking a rest.
The tides giggle softly, with bubbles and foam,
Inviting all creatures to make it their home!

Symphony of the Sea Breeze

A seagull croons to the waves' soft hum,
While crabs with their snacks go on a fun run.
Sea urchins dance, in the sand they do roll,
As plankton recite their most humorous scroll.

The dolphins pop popcorn, it's quite a delight,
While squids tell tall tales that stretch through the night.
With laughter and joy, the sea's in a trance,
As every critter joins in for the dance!

Kissed by the Tide

A crab wore a crown made of shell,
He danced like a king, all was well.
But seagulls had eyes for his royal flair,
They swooped in fast, oh, what a scare!

Fish played tag in a splashy parade,
While dolphins joked, their humor displayed.
A starfish grinned, trying to blend,
But beachgoers laughed, 'You don't really trend!'

Ebbing Lullabies

A clam sang softly, under the moon,
Bubbles joined in—what a weird tune!
A jellyfish giggled in shimmering light,
Tickled by waves, it danced through the night.

Seashells held secrets of messages old,
But crabs stole their gossip, so bold!
They snickered and chuckled all through the day,
As tides waved their hands, 'Come join in the play!'

Chasing Distant Horizons

A pirate with dreams of finding gold,
Chased fish on surfboards, strangely bold.
But instead of treasures, he found a fine whale,
Who winked and said, 'Matey, let's share a tail!'

Seagulls held meetings on driftwood high,
Discussing beach snacks while aiming for pie.
A pelican argued, 'I'm the best chef,'
But ended with sandwiches stuck to his left!

Waves Embrace of Stillness

A turtle so slow, with a bright pink tie,
Declared, 'I'm the leader, let's give it a try!'
But waves start to tickle, oh my what a sight,
He tumbled and giggled, oh what pure delight!

In the quiet, a starfish made a strange face,
'I'm the king of this rock, no need for a race!'
Yet when a crab raced by, quick as can be,
The starfish just sighed, 'Why won't they see me?'

Echoes of Forgotten Shores

Beneath the waves, where secrets hide,
The fish all gather, their fins open wide.
They whisper tales of shoes and hats,
While crabs do dances, all in spats.

Seagulls laugh, they swoop and dive,
Trying to steal a lunch—oh, what a jive!
The sandcastles wobble, then tumble down,
As a kid yells, "Hey! Not my crown!"

Lair of the Seafarers

Sailors sing from the saltiest bar,
Trading tall tales, 'I've caught a shark!'
But all they've caught is a soggy shoe,
Their raucous laughter echoes so true.

Their octopus friend, a terrible cook,
Pours jellyfish jelly in every nook.
They feast on plankton, and giggle with glee,
As one shouts, "More bread for my tea!"

Spellbound by the Sea

The tide rolls in with a bubbly cheer,
While turtles roll over, spread smiles so dear.
Seashells blush as crabs take a stroll,
One says to the other, "I'm on a roll!"

Mermaids giggle, their hair in a braid,
Juggling seaweed, a slippery trade.
With fish in a conga, they cha-cha and sway,
Who knew a shell could throw such a party today?

A Symphony of Salt and Surf

Waves crash in rhythm, a band on the beach,
With clams as trumpets, oh what a reach!
The dolphins swim in, a chorus so grand,
Announcing their concert across the sand.

But wait, a seagull steals the mic,
Yelling, "Back off, this is my hike!"
The crowd erupts, the sand begins to dance,
As everyone joins in, giving fun a chance.

Oceanic Ambiance

Waves giggle on the shore,
Tickling toes, what a chore!
Seagulls cawing, in a dance,
Crabs hold a sideways prance.

Sunbathers with their golden glow,
Sunscreen's struggle—a slippery show!
Flip-flops fly with all their might,
As a child makes a sandman's height.

Reverb of the Rock Pools

In a rock pool, a fish gets wise,
Wearing seashells as a disguise.
Tide pools bubbling, squeaky clean,
Crabs gossip like a teenage scene.

Starfish wave and pose with glee,
"Look at me, I'm fancy-free!"
Anemones dance, oh what a sight,
They bounce like they've had too much light.

Dance of the Rising Sun

Sun rises up, a giant yolk,
Seagulls holler like a bad joke.
Surfers stumble, wiping out,
They laugh and scream, "What's that about?"

Beach balls bounce and laughter swells,
A dog steals snacks, oh can't you tell?
Kids splash while parents sigh and frown,
Sandcastles built, then knocked right down.

Seashell Sonatas

Seashells play an ocean tune,
"Hey there, listen to our croon!"
A hermit crab joins in for fun,
Marching like a soldier on the run.

Waves clap hands like they're applauding,
While dolphins surf with joy, crooning.
A flip in the air, then down with a splash,
Seaweed wigs turned into a bash!

Twilight on the Shoreline

The waves they giggle, a playful surprise,
As seagulls squawk funny tunes in the skies.
Sandcastles wobble, then tumble down low,
While crabs dance a jig, putting on quite the show.

The sun takes a bow, wearing orange and red,
Shells gossip together, their secrets well-fed.
A fish with a hat swims by with a wink,
While starfish sit quietly, sipping on drink.

Stillness in the Swells

A beach ball drifts past, with no care at all,
It bounces on sea foam, then makes a loud call.
A snorkel-wearing dog dives down for a bone,
While floating on rafts, the kids start to moan.

The crabs, all in line, march forward with pride,
In search of their lunch, they squawk and they glide.
A dolphin nearby does silly flips and spins,
While the humans all laugh at the ocean's small wins.

The Marine Minuet

Octopus twirls in a suit and a tie,
While jellyfish waltz as they float on by.
A clam plays the flute, very off-key, you see,
While dolphins wear glasses, sipping cold tea.

The seaweed all sways in a very odd way,
As fish hold a party and invite the bay.
A whale makes a splash and soaks all the guests,
Their laughter erupts, much to their behests.

Crashing Silence

The waves whisper secrets, but giggle on pause,
As clowns in the tide tumble just for applause.
A fish with a mustache tricks folks on the shore,
While seashells play poker, who could ask for more?

A pelican fumbles, drops fries in the surf,
While sea turtles chuckle, still full of good mirth.
They dance with the foam and the sea spray divine,
As the sun sets softly, all feeling just fine.

Rhythms of the Misty Shore

Waves crash, clams scatter in fright,
Seagulls squawk, what a goofy sight!
A crab in a tux, looking quite dapper,
With pinchers raised high, he's quite the chapper.

Sunbathers burn, like toast in the sun,
While kids' sandcastles implode, oh what fun!
The breeze carries giggles, a joyous affair,
As rubber ducks float, without a care!

Luminescent Dreams in Tides

The jellyfish glow, a dance on the bay,
With tentacles wiggling, they sway and they play.
Fish in tuxedos swim past with flair,
While the shrimp in the corner can't help but stare.

A dolphin's splash makes the whole group cheer,
As starfish debate who's the best swimmer here.
Under the moon, they laugh and they gleam,
Together they ride on a magical dream!

Tranquility of Solitude

A hermit crab strolls, out of his shell,
He searched for a home, but he's doing quite well.
Seashells gossip, whispering sweet lies,
As the tide rolls in, they cover their sighs.

A lone pelican dives, misses its catch,
Splashing in chaos, but it'll try scratch.
The wind tells tales, oh how they amuse,
While the surf's gentle rhythm sings soft, happy blues!

Song of the Sea Glass

A seabird collects all the shiny bits bright,
He fashions a crown, dazzling under moonlight.
"Look at my treasure!" he croaks with a grin,
As fish roll their eyes, "Oh, buddy, where've you been?"

The sea foam pops like popcorn in play,
While sailors from yonder just sigh, "We'll stay."
They clink their mugs, toast to life's little charms,
As the shore whispers secrets, all held in its arms!

Playful Rhythms of Shells

Shells gather on the sandy floor,
Whispers of secrets, oh what a score!
Crabs dance sideways, in a funny parade,
While seagulls eye snacks, oh how they invade!

Waves clap their hands, like a jazz band,
Fish splash around, thinking it's all planned.
A dolphin hums tunes, oh so absurd,
While mermaids giggle, sharing a word!

Tidal Whispers

Waves tell jokes, but don't always land,
Gulls roll their eyes, it's all rather bland.
Tides ebb and flow, they've got good taste,
But don't ask a crab; they'll just growl and race!

Shimmering starlight, a splash of delight,
Fishes wear sunglasses, oh what a sight!
Starfish play poker, with shells laid out,
And clams just roll eyes; they know what it's about!

Blue Infinity Melodies

Mermaids sing loudly, off-key and proud,
While whales tell stories, echoing loud.
The jellyfish waltz, float like a kite,
But sea cucumbers just keep out of sight!

Sandy toes tap to the rhythm of waves,
Electric eels get shocked, oh how it chafes!
Coral reefs giggle, a colorful crew,
As octopuses juggle, just for a view!

Nightfall on the Waters

As the sun dips low, the stars pop like corn,
Crickets chirp tunes, 'til the very morn.
Frogs croak a symphony, quite out of tune,
While turtles play tag, racing under the moon!

Bubbles rise up, like laughter, they soar,
And fish wear top hats, begging for more.
Seashells play maracas, all night long,
In this watery world, where all sing along!

The Calm Before the Swell

In the stillness, waves do tease,
Seagulls squawk as if to please.
A lobster cracks a silly joke,
While on the shore, a sea sponge croak.

Sandcastles rise with royal flair,
A crab in shoes, debonair.
The tide rolls in, a gentle push,
While fish play tag, in a frisky hush.

Verses of the Water's Edge

At the water's edge, I lost my hat,
A fish now wears it, imagine that!
Waves tickle toes and splash about,
While dolphins giggle, jumping out.

A beach ball rolls, takes a leap,
As children laugh and seagulls peep.
The sun's warm grin, a golden tease,
As sand drifts in like slow-falling leaves.

Murmurs of Forgotten Shores

Hidden whispers in the tide,
A seashell's tale, a secret guide.
The crabs put on a dance so fine,
While turtles waddle, sipping brine.

Old fish gossip in bubbles clear,
Sardines escape without a fear.
A starfish grins, it's quite a sight,
Underwater, laughter takes flight.

The Sea's Hidden Heartbeat

Beneath the waves, a secret beat,
Fishes prance with flapping feet.
An octopus paints with great delight,
While seaweed giggles in the night.

A dolphin dives in a silly spin,
As mermaids laugh, their cheeks a-grin.
With every splash, a joke unfurls,
The sea's a stage, where fun whirls.

Harmonies in the Abyss

Fish are dancing in a waltz,
Sardines shaking without a fault.
Octopuses twist with flair,
While clams just sit and stare.

Crabs are cranking up the beat,
With wiggly tails and tiny feet.
A shark joins in, a noble sight,
But slips and lands, oh what a fright!

Mollusks hum a jazzy tune,
Underneath the silver moon.
Starfish clap with all their might,
As seaweeds sway left and right.

But the whale just wants to nap,
While the jellyfish does a tap.
In such a bubbly serenade,
Who can resist this frothy parade?

Tranquil Currents

Waves are whispering silly jokes,
As dolphins leap with happy hoax.
The sea turtles roll their eyes,
While seagulls plot their next surprise.

Sandcastles crumble with a crash,
As kids all run for a quick splash.
Starfish pull a funny face,
As water tickles all in place.

Seashells giggle on the shore,
Telling tales of ocean lore.
But when the tide begins to rise,
They hide away with soft goodbyes.

In this realm where laughs collide,
The sea life plays, with joy and pride.
Each wave a chuckle, soft and light,
Making even crabs dance with delight.

Cryptic Rhythms of the Coast

The sands are singing, grains in tune,
Crabs doing dances, such a boon!
Walruses breathe their deep refrain,
While sea cows play a silly game.

A clam belts out a xylophone,
And fish throw parties with a drone.
But the mermaids, oh so sly,
Are busy crafting cakes to fry.

Anemones flaunt their colors bright,
As seahorses twirl in pure delight.
With seafoam giggles in the spray,
They splash their worries all away.

Echoes of laughter fill the air,
With every wave that meets the flare.
In this underwater carnival,
Even the rocks have fun after all!

Beneath the Surface

Bubbles pop like little cheers,
As squids celebrate their years.
Seahorses prance in silly gear,
While nudibranchs shed a tear.

Turtles complain about slow pace,
While eels twist and stake their place.
Shrimps break out in silly song,
Bobbing along, they can't go wrong.

Pufferfish blow up with glee,
As they groove with carefree spree.
But when the school of fish moves in,
The jellies start to swing and grin.

In the depths, where giggles float,
Every creature learns to gloat.
A funny world beneath the tide,
Where joy and laughter can't subside.

Ripples of Reflection

In the water, a fish does a dance,
With a crab that thinks he has a chance.
They twirl and they spin, what a sight to see,
Until the seagull dives, and they flee with glee.

A starfish lounges, soaking up rays,
Wondering why he's not in the fray.
He can't move fast, it's a funny plight,
While sea urchins giggle, 'Oh, what a sight!'

Sounds of the Solitude

The waves whisper secrets, oh what a tease,
A clam's quite a gossip, as happy as you please.
He shares silly tales of the shrimp and their prance,
While seaweed just sways, lost in a trance.

A whale hums a tune, out of tune it may be,
And dolphins join in for a watery spree.
They laugh at the plankton who bounces along,
Making music so weird, it feels oh so wrong!

Tide's Gentle Embrace

The tide rolls in, with a bubbly grin,
Saltwater tickles, can't help but grin.
A jellyfish wobbles, like a floating balloon,
As sandcastles crumble, their fate's coming soon.

Seagulls dive down for a snack on the go,
But end up with seaweed, oh what a show!
They squawk and they squabble, what chaos unfurls,
While kids on the beach toss sand in swirls.

Notes from the Nautilus

In a shell on the ocean floor, tunes start to play,
A nautilus sings in a quirky way.
He plucks at the seaweed, strumming with flair,
While crabs tap their claws, joining in the air.

With barnacles bobbing, they form a nice band,
Drifting and jiving, making music so grand.
The ocean's the stage for this comical show,
Where laughter and melody happily flow.

Swells of Reflection

I sat on a boat, feeling quite grand,
With seagulls dancing, a wobbly band.
My sandwich flew off, like a fish in the sky,
It's hard to eat lunch when the snacks say goodbye.

The waves chuckle softly, a sea-salt jest,
Where mermaids swim in their curious quest.
A crab on the deck does the cha-cha with flair,
While I try to balance, pretending I care.

Glimmers in the Wave

A starfish once told me, 'Stop stretching your arms!'
'You're scaring the fish with your silly charms!'
But the dolphins just giggled, they're always so keen,
To play in the bubbles, all shiny and clean.

With flip-flops in hand, I made a big splash,
Till I tripped on a jelly and ended in a crash.
The beachcombers chuckled, their laughter like gold,
As I flailed in the water, my dignity sold.

Rhythmic Breaths of the Bay

The tide whispered secrets in hushed, silly tones,
While seaweed danced, like a jester in moans.
I tried to take notes on the songs of the sea,
But the tide kept on tickling, oh, let me be free!

A whale took a bow, with a splash and a grin,
Singing off-key, like a chorus of tin.
I laughed 'til I snorted, then fell off my chair,
Who knew the deep blue held such silly flair?

Phantom Melodies of the Sea

The ghost of a pirate, sipping on brine,
Sang shanties that were utterly out of line.
With a parrot named Squawk who would squawk on repeat,
They turned my beach trip into a comic treat.

As I searched for the treasure, I dug with great glee,
Found a bottle of sunscreen, no gold as I see.
But the laughter of waves kept my spirits so high,
In this whimsical world, I was ready to fly.

Chords of the Endless Horizon

The seagull's squawk in perfect tune,
As crabs dance under the silver spoon.
A fish in a bow tie takes the stage,
While the octopus flirts, quite the outrage!

Waves clap their hands to the beat of the sun,
As dolphins play tag, oh what fun!
The clam conducts with a witty shell,
And jellyfish glow, casting their spell.

Sandcastles crumble like soggy dreams,
While flip-flops squeak in silly screams.
The tide rolls in, a playful tease,
As crabs crack jokes, laughing with ease!

With every splash, a giggling cheer,
Nature's concert, oh so dear.
Join the fun with a surfboard ride,
In this seaside symphony, let's coincide!

Harmonies of the Deep Blue

A whale in a hat sings with flair,
While the tuna tap dances, oh so rare.
The seaweed sways, a groovy sight,
And the stingray glides, what pure delight!

Crustaceans rave in their funky shells,
As starfish spin tales and funny yells.
The bubbles rise in a jazzy swirl,
While clowns fish grin and give a twirl.

Anemones waltz with a rhythmic grace,
And fish in bow ties join the race.
The corals giggle as they sway,
In the underwater ball, come what may!

A hermit crab stumbles in a jive,
As mermen groove, feel alive!
Whimsical tunes fill the blue embrace,
Dance to the beat in this vibrant space!

Stillness in the Swell

The lazy tide hums a gentle tune,
While lazy sea lions munch on prunes.
A clam snores softly, nestled in sand,
While the sea cucumbers form a band!

The starfish stretch in a sunny wink,
As plankton parties, don't you think?
A sea turtle suits up for the ball,
With a bow on his shell, he's ready to enthrall!

Drifting thoughts on a breezy day,
With seaweed decorations in disarray.
The ocean's laugh echoes from afar,
As gulls play charades on a driftwood bar!

Fish gossip under the silver moon,
As crabs arm wrestle, oh, what a swoon!
Even in calm, there's unpredictable fun,
In these playful waves, we're never done!

Ballad of the Ocean Depths

Beneath the waves, where the laughter flows,
An octopus juggles with his toes.
A dolphin leaps, wearing sunglasses bright,
While squids do pirouettes in the moonlight!

The anchovies sing in an opera voice,
Encouraging each fish to rejoice.
With bubbles bursting in a jolly spree,
The depths become a circus of glee!

The sea floor plays host to a dance-off,
With each move, the crustaceans scoff.
Corals applaud with polypy hands,
In this underwater world, fun expands!

The pirate ship's ghost winks from afar,
As mermaids giggle, wishing on a star.
With a wink and a splash, let the fun unfold,
In the depths where stories of laughter are told!

Quiet Reflections on Water

Waves giggle as they break,
Fish wear socks, make no mistake.
Salty seaweed floats around,
Dancing shoes on sandy ground.

Seagulls squawk a silly tune,
Clams are tapping like a loon.
Crabs are plotting near the shore,
Silly critters, who'd want more?

Drifting boats with silly sails,
A cat stealing all the meals.
Turtles wearing tiny hats,
Do they think they're urban cats?

Ebbing tides just take a break,
Wave ride loops, some funny shakes.
Splashing laughter, sea's delight,
Watch the fish jump in their flight.

Hymn to the Horizon

Clouds are puffy, white and round,
Sailing on the air, so sound.
Sailors sing to sewing nets,
In the wind, their laughs are set.

Kites are dancing, runs are free,
Windy mishaps, oh golly gee!
Catch a breeze and make a wish,
Then drown the fish with a swish.

Sunset's hues in shaky lines,
Fishermen's great pranks with pines.
Jellyfish with floppy jests,
Wobbling like old dancing quests.

Dolphins jump, they cheer and tease,
Riding waves with style and ease.
Marine life has a comic flair,
Underwater, they're a rare pair.

Resounding Serenity of the Depths

Bubbles pop with silly sounds,
Octopus in shades confounds.
Silly fish in disco lights,
Grooving to the silent sites.

Underwater, laughter's free,
Blowfish puff, what could they be?
Crabs in tuxes on parade,
Making memories that won't fade.

Seahorses dance with graceful flair,
Swaying softly in cool air.
Eel's against the current glee,
Comedic moments in the sea.

Tides are playing hide and seek,
Coral secrets make us peek.
Voices echo, quite a shift,
Nature's bounty, funny gift.

Lull of the Lagoon

Lagoon's laughter, soft and light,
Crickets chirp, the moon is bright.
Frogs are croaking, what a din,
With each leap, they start to spin.

Water lilies wear their crowns,
Bouncing droplets, silly clowns.
Egrets strut with puffed-up pride,
In their dance, they take a ride.

Mice in boats with tiny oars,
Racing dreams on rich seashores.
Cattails waving like good friends,
Join the fun till daylight ends.

Cows by the edge grace the scene,
Mooing songs, where fish have been.
Laughter echoes, quirks abound,
In the lagoon, joy is found.

Peaceful Waters' Reverie

A fish forgot its sunglasses,
Swam straight into a jellyfish.
He cried out, "What a blunder!"
But laughed bubbles without a wish.

The seagulls laugh in their flight,
Imitating silly frogs.
The waves are clapping with glee,
As crabs dance on their logs.

A mermaid combs her hair with pride,
While a clam just takes a nap.
The dolphins juggle seaweed balls,
In this underwater trap.

All creatures sway to unseen tunes,
With sandcastles smiling bright.
They twirl and twist in the blue,
Underneath the sun's warm light.

Notes from the Nautilus

In a shell upon the sand,
A snail sends notes by sea breeze.
"Dear fish, stop being so grand,
You swim with utmost ease!"

Octopus writes a quirky rhyme,
With ink that dances on the waves.
"Don't mind me, I'm just biding time,
While sea stars dine on sea caves!"

The sea cucumber shakes its head,
"Why don't you guys just relax?"
But all of them just dance instead,
In colorful, silly knick-knacks.

A kraken dreams of jellybeans,
As bubbles float in doom.
"Oh, why can't life be kinder, please?
Instead of being a gloopy gloom!"

Solitude of the Surf

The tide whispers jokes to the shore,
Where turtles chuckle alone.
Seashells giggle on the floor,
While crabs throw stones in their zone.

Waves ask the rocks to share a tale,
But rocks just quietly stare.
"C'mon, let's not go pale,
It's not like you've got hair!"

Seahorses dance with flair and spin,
While plankton plot a new trend.
"Let's wear hats made of thin skin,
To celebrate summer's end!"

The ocean chuckles, rolls its eyes,
At antics so absurd.
"If only wisdom came as pies,
Then all would fly like birds!"

Voice of the Seafoam

The foam shouts puns that tickle fins,
As seastars roll on their backs.
"Why did the fish swim with grins?
He forgot he had no snacks!"

Nudibranchs giggle, peeling slow,
As shells play hopscotch on the sand.
"Oh look, a sailing seaweed show,
That's something we never planned!"

Fish ride back on bubbles of joy,
And sea urchins start a band.
"We'll groove and bounce, a new ploy,
While eels twist to their own brand!"

As laughter echoes near and far,
The ocean's heart beats fast.
With every wave, a new bizarre,
For fun is meant to last!

Under the Veil of Waves

Bubbles rise and giggles splash,
Fish in bow ties make a dash,
Turtles tease in slow-mo grace,
While seaweed dances, takes their place.

A crab in shades joins the parade,
With every snap, a joke is laid,
The starfish claps its five small hands,
As laughter ripples through the sands.

Octopus with ink so bright,
Draws mustaches with delight,
In this underwater cafe scene,
Everyone's a silly queen.

So raise a glass of salted air,
To all the fun that's down in there,
With happy critters humbly glow,
While currents carry on the show.

Threnody of the Current

Waves are jesters in a play,
Tickling boats that float away,
Seagulls cackle with delight,
As they dive in the coastal flight.

A dolphin flips with comical flair,
While fish gossip without a care,
Anemones do the cha-cha slide,
In this dance, there's nothing to hide.

A clam with pearls is quite the show,
Telling tales of long ago,
While crabs try to steal the scene,
Sporting socks that are bright green.

Oh, what a symphony we weave,
In the waves where we believe,
Life's just one big ocean jest,
And we all float in the best quest.

Rhythms of the Rolling Deep

Beneath the surface, laughter swells,
Coral castles, untold tales,
A fish in jeans and cap asks, "Why?"
And bubbles pop with a cheerful sigh.

The tides may roll, but joy won't stop,
As plankton dance and jelly swap,
A whale with a wig sings off-key,
In this gala for all to see.

When currents join in a rippling beat,
Even the barnacles tap their feet,
Clownfish joke and truly thrive,
In this realm where all are alive.

So let the sea breeze blow you along,
With barnacles humming a catchy song,
As laughter echoes in the swell,
In the whirlpool, where joys compel.

Fluid Whisperings

Secrets swirl in salty tails,
As underwater folly prevails,
A crab cracks jokes about the tide,
While shrimp parade, full of pride.

A sea sponge caught in a swirl,
Wiggles around, giving a twirl,
Fish in bowties join the fun,
In a party that's never done.

A narwhal with spectacles reads,
The ocean floor's gossiping needs,
Sea stars giggle, a light so bright,
Under starlit waves, what a sight!

So dance along with fins and flippers,
And laugh with the gills as the sea shippers,
In liquid laughter, let it unfold,
With every wave, a story told.

The Call of the Aqua

The waves are laughing, what a hoot,
A fish in sunglasses, lookin' cute.
Seagulls juggling chips in the air,
While crabs dance funny, without a care.

Splashing around, the tides do tease,
A mermaid grins, under the breeze.
Shells are chatting, gossip so grand,
While starfish are doing the conga on sand.

Echoing Horizons

The dolphins are giggling, oh what a sight,
Riding the waves, in pure delight.
Octopuses juggle with eight wiggly arms,
While sea turtles compete in silly charms.

A crab in a top hat, oh so dapper,
Beware of the waves, don't take a napper.
The seaweed is dancing, swaying so free,
Under the surface where fish swim with glee.

Twilight's Shoreline Song

Moonlit giggles from bumping surf,
A squid with a trumpet sends laughs forth.
Seashells echo tales with a twist,
While starfish pose as stylists, you get the gist.

The tide brings whispers of jokes in the mist,
A whale in a bow tie adds to the list.
Sandcastles crumble with laughter and cheer,
As the tide rolls in, their fate's made clear.

Beneath Celestial Waters

Bubbles rise up, each with a grin,
Fish wearing bowties dive right in.
A lobster plays poker, stakes are high,
While jellyfish float, giving a sigh.

Plankton are partying, just one more round,
With shaky little moves that astound.
The sea urchins chatter with bashful delight,
In this playful world, everything feels right.

The Enchanted Foam

Always dancing, light as air,
The bubbles laugh without a care.
They tickle toes and splash around,
In playful tricks, their joy is found.

Seagulls squawk with such delight,
Chasing waves, a comical sight.
A crab in shoes starts to prance,
He's got the moves to make you dance!

Starfish wearing tiny hats,
Pose for selfies with the spats.
Little fish in bow ties swim,
Their underwater revelry, a whim!

So when you stroll along the shore,
Just listen close, there's so much more.
The giggles and the splashes sing,
The beach is where the fun takes wing!

Mystique of the Murmuring Sea

A dolphin's grin, a cheeky ploy,
Playing tag with waves of joy.
A pirate's hat falls from his head,
He'll retake it, not be misled.

Waves that ripple, chuckles loud,
They form a very giggly crowd.
The seaweed sways, a funny dance,
It's the latest fashion, take a chance!

Shells that whisper silly rhymes,
In salty lingo, naughts and chimes.
Each splash, a giggle to the shore,
Someone's boat flips—what's in store?

Laughing waters, play the part,
With every wave, they steal a heart.
So join the fun, come take a dive,
In this mystique, we come alive!

Whispers of the Deep

Listen close, the sea has jokes,
Fishy faces, swarming folks.
Octopuses with arms so long,
Best at tug-of-war, oh so strong!

The clam tries hard to keep a grin,
But every time, he just won't win.
With every shell, a comedic scene,
As crabs look on, not too serene.

Turtles stroll in shoes too big,
They take their time, always a gig.
A whale's deep laugh can shake the sea,
Crack a joke, and they all agree!

So down below, the fun's so neat,
In bubbles bright, they skip to greet.
With whispers soft, they'll surely cheer,
Funny tides bring laughter here!

Melody of Tides

The tides hum tunes of joy and glee,
As jellyfish sway with casual spree.
A fish holds high a tiny flag,
While eels dance by with a comic wag.

Seashells chirp their playful sounds,
With every pulse, laughter abounds.
Salted air lifts spirits high,
As waves tickle the clouds in the sky.

Sea cucumbers sport funky hats,
While fish tease tiny, dancing gnats.
A crab's cartwheel defies all sense,
He falls, but his joys make recompense!

Every splash and every flip,
Turns serious thoughts into a quip.
Embrace the song, join the ride,
In this melody, let fun abide!

Whispers of the Deep

A fish wore a hat, quite a sight,
With a wink and a grin, he'd take flight.
He danced with the crabs on a rock,
While turtles rolled by with a tick-tock.

The shells had a gossip, oh so grand,
About bubbles that burst at sea's band.
Seahorses laughed at a clumsy clam,
Who tried to sing like a seafaring jam.

The seaweed would sway, in rhythm so neat,
As a starfish played marbles, oh what a feat!
A dolphin jumped high with a joke in tow,
While jellyfish giggled, enjoying the show.

So if you dive deep where the sea dragons dwell,
You'll find that the ocean's got stories to tell.
In laughter and joy, it's a vast wavy spree,
With a splash of humor, oh come play with me!

Secrets Beneath the Waves

Under the foam where the sea cucumbers hide,
A clam made a wish with a wink and a slide.
Pufferfish giggled, puffed out for a jest,
While crabs in bow ties were dressed at their best.

An octopus spun tales with eight hands,
About the weird world of night sand castles and bands.
A starfish played chess with a stubborn old log,
While an eel sang softly, wrapped round in a fog.

The sand at the bottom held secrets galore,
Of pirates who danced and frolicked on shore.
The currents sent tickles through fish in a line,
As they joked and they jived, oh what a fine time!

So listen intently, if you dare take a look,
The secrets are rich as a well-read book.
With laughter and joy, let your heart be the wave,
In the dance of the deep, find the fun that we crave!

Lullabies from the Abyss

Deep in the blue, where the sun barely glows,
A clownfish hummed tunes, twirling in prose.
With bubbles like confetti, and a flip of the tail,
He serenaded the sharks with a curious tale.

The turtles rolled over, a giggling delight,
As sea urchins bounced in a dance of moonlight.
A whale gave a sigh that sounded quite fab,
While sardines formed crowds, playing tag in the lab.

The octopuses drummed on some old barnacles,
Throwing parties for all, with small hearticles.
Anemones swayed, their tentacles will,
As they joined in the music, their joy couldn't fill.

So drift in the depths where the echoes are deep,
Let the lullabies whisper, as they softly sweep.
With a wink and a wave, let's join in the throng,
In the rhythm of laughter, we all sing along!

Echoes of the Tides

The tide rolled in with a bouncy little cheer,
As crabs clapped their claws, with surges of beer.
A mermaid with style flipped her tail with glee,
Singing songs of the sea, like we're wild and free!

Seagulls with flair, dressed up for a show,
Dive-bombing fish with a comedic flow.
The kelp danced a jig, waving hands in the breeze,
Making waves of delight, as they tickled the seas.

A shark in a tux, oh what a surprise,
He twirled and he whirled, under oceanic skies.
While dolphins were laughing, sharing tales in a race,
With hydrangeas swaying, joining in with grace.

So come take a dip in this bubbly embrace,
Where laughter plays tag, and fun finds its place.
In the echoes of tides, where the currents are strong,
The sea's got a party, so come sing along!

Ballad of the Blue

There once was a fish with a thinker's frown,
He pondered since morning, now he's upside down.
His friends joked and laughed as they swam by,
"Life's a big wave, time to just ride high!"

The shells had a party, a seaweed band,
They danced on the sand until they couldn't stand.
A crab tried to waltz but got stuck to a shoe,
He shouted, "Help, I'm trapped! Come rescue me too!"

So the starfish played DJ with jellyfish lights,
While seagulls engaged in high-flying fights.
They flapped and they squawked as they stole all the fries,

While the fish just rolled by with a look of surprise.

Then a whale blew a bubble that floated and glowed,
It popped with a splash, and the laughter just flowed.
In the depths of the blue, where the silliness thrived,
All creatures agreed, it's a blast to be alive!

The Sea's Hidden Chorus

Under the waves, where the laughter resounds,
A clam and a snail found some jazz underground.
They formed a trio, with a crab on the beat,
The sea sponge said, "Man, this is quite the treat!"

Octopus tapping with eight funky limbs,
The sea cucumbers joined in with their whims.
They jived and they boogied on the ocean floor,
While fish flew by; they couldn't take it anymore.

The dolphins, they flipped, with a splash and a twist,
"Come groove with us, you won't want to miss!"
But the shark just grinned, with a plan in his smile,
"I'm here for the fun, and I'll stay for a while!"

But laughter erupted when a wave came too fast,
And the whole party zapped, oh how it was cast!
With bubbles and giggles, they swirled in the brine,
In the sea's hidden chorus, they sang and they shined!

Murmurs of the Driftwood

A piece of driftwood said, "What a life I live!"
"I float on the tide, always willing to give."
"I've seen some wild things: a sock, maybe two,
And once, for a moment, a whole lost shoe!"

With barnacles chatting on the wood's old tie,
They laughed at the currents as they drifted by.
"You think you're so smooth with your smooth-polished plank?
But I've caught a ride on a fish with a crank!"

One seagull swooped down with a question so odd,
"Hey driftwood buddy, why do you nod?"
"I murmur with waves, in the breezy sunbeam,
In the heart of the sea, I'm living the dream!"

So they laughed as they floated on the gentle swell,
With whispers and giggles, they cast quite a spell.
In the driftwood's realm, where the funny times reign,
All creatures conspired: let's drift back again!

Undercurrents of Emotion

A dolphin once sighed, saying, "Oh what a day!"
"I swam past a seal, who had nothing to say!"
"The crabs were all grumpy, and the sturgeons stood still,

Yet a clownfish was clowning, spreading laughter at will!"

In the still of the deep, emotions ran high,
A shark in a tuxedo went out for a fry.
He danced with the rays; they twirled through the gloom,
While the flounder just hid, planning his own boom!

The seaweed was swaying, feeling quite spry,
With currents of giggles that floated on by.
A grouper exclaimed, "Hey, let's throw a bash,
I've got the sea-bass, and we'll make quite the splash!"

So the reef held a banquet, a feast under stars,
With jellyfish lanterns and crab-filled jars.
They laughed and they cried, with a splash of delight,
In the undercurrents of joy, they danced through the night

Tides of Tranquility

The tide rolled in, it stole my shoe,
My toes are now wet, oh what a view!
Crabs dance by, in a little parade,
Who knew the beach was a stage for charades?

Seagulls are squawking, they want my fries,
They eye my lunch with crafty spies.
I laugh and wave as they swoop and dive,
In this sandy circus, I feel so alive!

A beach ball bounces, it lands on my head,
Just when I thought I could relax in bed!
The sun plays tricks, with shadows it weaves,
But who needs shade? It's fun, I believe!

The wave's a tease, it splashes and runs,
Chasing my laughter, oh what a bunch!
As I slip and slide, in this salty spree,
The beach is the place where I'm wild and free!

Enchanted Shores

Once upon a time, on a sunny shore,
I found a shell, but it's not a bore.
It whispered secrets of pirate gold,
But turned out to be just a story retold.

Jellyfish float like they own the scene,
I tiptoe around, feeling quite green.
With umbrellas bright like a rainbow's end,
We dance in the sun, our shadows pretend.

The waves giggle softly, a musical beat,
While flip-flops play tag on sandy retreat.
I chased a seagull, thought I could fly,
But it just looked back with a knowing eye.

On enchanted shores, laughter spills free,
Nature's own joke is just waiting for me.
A sprinkle of salt, a splash of delight,
In the chaos of fun, I'm ready for flight!

The Poetic Pulse of the Sea

The sea hums a tune on its way to the sand,
While I try to juggle with ice cream in hand.
It drips and it drops, like a messy parade,
I laugh at the chaos my sweet tooth has made.

Crabs doing limbo, oh what a sight,
They wave their claws like a festive invite.
I join in the dance with a slip and a slide,
The humor of nature I can't seem to hide.

A fish with a bowtie swims right by me,
He winks with a fin, oh what could it be?
I throw him a wink, he flips with a grin,
In this wavy world, it's laughter that wins.

As the tide rolls in, it's a comic relief,
Where joy splashes high, like a bright ocean thief.
With each frothy wave, the playful seas laugh,
And leave us to ponder, just who's in charge of this craft?

Lightly Touched by the Sea Breeze

The sea breeze tickles my nose with a sigh,
As I build a sandcastle that's three stories high.
But a wave comes crashing, my tower's in dread,
Guess it's back to the drawing board, I said!

A dolphin jumps high, it flips with such glee,
I shout in delight, oh look at me!
Splashing around, like I'm part of the crew,
Even the sandbars can't hold my view.

Kites swirling high, they dance with the sun,
But every gust takes them off on the run.
I chase them and tumble, a sight sure to see,
And laugh at my antics, the ocean's decree.

As night falls gently, with stars in the sky,
I sit on the shore and let out a sigh.
For the laughter and joy will never cease,
In the gentle embrace of my sandy piece!

www.ingramcontent.com/pod-product-compliance
Lightning Source LLC
Chambersburg PA
CBHW070326120526
44590CB00017B/2822